The Sword of Abram

N. D. Wilson
illustrated by Forrest Dickison

THE OLD STORIES
canonpress
Moscow, Idaho

THE OLD STORIES

The Dragon and the Garden
In the Time of Noah
The Sword of Abram

N. D. Wilson, *The Sword of Abram*
Paperback edition published October 2016.
Text copyright © 2014, 2016 by N. D. Wilson
Illustrations copyright © 2014, 2016 by Forrest Dickison

Published by Canon Press, P.O. Box 8729, Moscow, ID 83843
800–488–2034 | www.canonpress.com

19 20 21   5 4 3 2

Cover and interior design by Laura Blakey. Layout by James Engerbretson.
Printed in the United States of America.

Library of Congress Cataloging-in-Publication Data is available.

ISBN-10: 1-944503-78-1
ISBN-13: 978-1-944503-78-9

For Shadrach
NDW

For Kekoa
FD

Abram was a man who had no land and no sons. The world was fresh again after the Flood, and peoples had spread through it according to their languages and built themselves kingdoms and cities.

Abram was rich in silver and gold, and rich in his herds, but he roamed, and his kingdom was a tent.

Abram's nephew Lot roamed with him, and their herds and their families and all the men and women in their households traveled with them.

But they were not at peace. Together their herds were too large for the land and the men who tended the animals warred over every pasture and every spring.

Abram took his nephew and together they walked through the land.

"We are blood," Abram said, "and there should be no strife between us. Separate your household from mine, and choose land for yourself. If you go to the right, then I will go left. If you choose the left, then I will dwell on the right."

Lot looked over the land and saw the lush valley of the Jordan, and five cities stood on the green plains around it. The greatest was called Sodom, which was a wicked place.

"That will be my land," Lot said. "I will dwell in the cities of the plains and pitch my tents toward Sodom."

When Lot was gone, Abram walked to a high place to see where he should go. There the Lord spoke to him.

"You have no land," the Lord said. "But look to the north and to the south, to the east and to the west. All that you see I will give to you and to your people."

Abram heard the Lord, but he had no sons.

Then a wind came and swirled the dust at Abram's feet into a great cloud.

"When a man can number the dust," the Lord said, "then your children shall be numbered."

Abram heard, but he did not yet believe.

In those days, while Abram roamed, there was a great king in the land of Elam called Chedorlaomer. He was powerful, and many weaker kings owed him gold and silver.

Together, the king of Sodom and the kings from the cities of the plains decided to rebel against Chedorlaomer. Before their people, they swore to send him no more tribute, and they called up their armies to overthrow him.

Other peoples rebelled as well—the Rephaim and the Zuzim, who were strong like the sons of giants, and their allies with them.

Chedorlaomer was angry. Three kings still served him and together they raised up a great army.

The four kings rode out in a swarm of chariots with their strongest fighters riding on long-legged horses beside them.

Behind the horses and chariots came thousands of soldiers on foot, archers and men with spears, and a great caravan of wagons and camels carrying food and tents.

First, the army of Chedorlaomer fell on the mighty Rephaim and Zuzim.

The sun shone on the bronze armor of Chedorlaomer's men as they swirled around their enemy and cut the great ones down.

The men who had walked like sons of giants were left on the field to fill the bellies of young lions and every scavenger in the wilds.

Chedorlaomer did not rest but turned his chariot toward Sodom and the cities of the plains.

The king of Sodom, and the four kings with him, rode out with their armies to the valley of Siddim, a dangerous place full of bogs and slime.

There they the met the anger of Chedorlaomer.

The armies from the plains met the men of Chedorlaomer and were destroyed. Thousands fell, and as the king of Sodom fled the fast arrows of his enemies, his chariot toppled into a slimepit and he was killed.

Chedorlaomer killed all the rebel kings and sent his men to Sodom and the other cities. There they took rich fabrics, herds, gold, and men and women for slaves.

There they took Lot, the son of Abram's brother.

When Abram heard his nephew had been taken as a slave, he called together all the men born in his household, his trained servants.

Three hundred and eighteen mounted camels, and he armed them with bows and curved bronze swords.

Then Abram spoke: "Though Chedorlaomer is a king of kings and I am a king of tents and sheep, the Lord will give him to us and we will cut him down."

Then they set off after Chedorlaomer, Abram at the head of his three hundred.

Abram came to Chedorlaomer's army at night. The soldiers were laughing and drinking in their tents, unafraid of any enemy, for there were no more armies to face them.

Abram divided his three hundred, and they rode into the camp from every side and overran the great army.

Three hundred killed thousands and Abram struck down Chedorlaomer outside his tent.

Then Abram found Lot and brought him back, along with all the men and women and animals and the other goods of Sodom.

Melchizedek, a priest and king of Salem, rode out to meet Abram, and the new king of Sodom came with him.

"Return only the people," the king of Sodom said, "but keep all the gold, and the animals, and the rich fabrics for yourself."

"No," Abram said, "Sodom is a wicked place. I will keep nothing of yours, not even a lace for my sandal, or you would say, 'I made Abram rich.'"

Then Melchizedek laughed.

"I have a gift for Abram, servant of the Most High God," he said. And Abram knelt before the great priest-king, and Melchizedek gave him bread and wine and placed his hand on Abram's head.

"Blessed be Abram," he said, "possessor of heaven and earth, and blessed be the Most High God, who delivered your enemies into your hand."

And Abram gave Melchizedek great riches, a tenth of all he had.

After these things, Abram slept, and the Lord came to him in a vision.

"Fear not, Abram," the Lord said. "I am your shield and your great reward."

"What will you give me?" Abram asked, "for I have no children?"

And the Lord caught him up out of his tent and showed him the night sky.

"Look into Heaven," the Lord said. "Speak with the stars and count them if you can. So shall your children be."

And Abram believed.